CONTEMPORARY AMERICAN SUCCESS STORIES

Famous People of Hispanic Heritage

Volume II

Barbara J. Marvis

A Mitchell Lane
Multicultural Biography Series
• Celebrating Diversity •

CONTEMPORARY AMERICAN SUCCESS STORIES
Famous People of Hispanic Heritage

<table>
<tr><td>

VOLUME I
Geraldo Rivera
Melissa Gonzalez
Federico Peña
Ellen Ochoa
</td><td>

**VOLUME II
Tommy Nuñez
Margarita Esquiroz
Cesar Chavez
Antonia Novello**
</td><td>

VOLUME III
Giselle Fernandez
Jon Secada
Desi Arnaz
Joan Baez
</td><td>

VOLUME IV
Selena Quintanilla Pérez
Robert Rodriguez
Josefina López
Alfredo Estrada
</td><td>

VOLUME V
Gloria Estefan
Fernando Cuza
Rosie Perez
Cheech Marin
</td></tr>
<tr><td>

VOLUME VI
Pedro José Greer
Nancy Lopez
Rafael Palmeiro
Hilda Perera
</td><td>

VOLUME VII
Raul Julia
Mariah Carey
Andres Galarraga
Mary Joe Fernandez
</td><td>

VOLUME VIII
Cristina Saralegui
Trent Dimas
Nydia Velázquez
Jimmy Smits
</td><td>

VOLUME IX
Roy Benavidez
Isabel Allende
Oscar De La Hoya
Jackie Guerra
</td><td>

VOLUME X
Rebecca Lobo
Carlos Mencia
Linda Chavez Thompson
Bill Richardson
</td></tr>
</table>

Publisher's Cataloging in Publication
Marvis, Barbara J.
    Famous people of Hispanic heritage. Vol. II / Barbara J. Marvis.

    p. cm. —(Contemporary American success stories)—(A Mitchell Lane multicultural biography series)
    Includes index.
    LCCN: 95-75963
    ISBN: 1-883845-23-8 (hc)
    ISBN: 1-883845-22-X (pbk)

    1. Hispanic Americans—Biography—Juvenile literature. I. Title. II. Series.

E184.S75M37 1996

920'.009268
QBI96-20404

Illustrated by Barbara Tidman
Project Editor: Susan R. Scarfe

Mitchell Lane PUBLISHERS

Your Path To Quality Educational Material
P. O. Box 200
Childs, Maryland 21916-0200

TABLE OF CONTENTS

Acknowledgments

Every reasonable effort has been made to seek copyright permission, where such permission has been deemed necessary. Any oversight brought to the publisher's attention will be corrected in future printings.

Most of the stories in this series were written through personal interviews and/or with the complete permission of the person, representative of, or family of the person being profiled, and are authorized biographies. Though we attempted to personally contact each and every person profiled within, for various reasons we were unable to authorize every story. All stories have been thoroughly researched and checked for accuracy, and to the best of our knowledge represent true stories.

We wish to acknowledge with gratitude the generous cooperation of Tommy Nuñez (telephone interview April 25, 1995) and Mary Ann Nuñez in the compilation of the story about and photographs of Tommy Nuñez; Tom Featherstone, Abraham Bonowitz, the Cesar E. Chavez Foundation, Marc Grossman, the United Farm Workers, and the Walter P. Reuther Library for help with our story about and photographs of Cesar Chavez; Margarita Esquiroz (telephone interview May 16, 1995) and Delia Lopez Francis for help with our story of Margarita Esquiroz. We also wish to express our sincere thanks to Elaine DagenBela of the Hispanic Heritage Awards for her recommendations as to those we have profiled.

Photograph Credits

The quality of the photographs in this book may vary; many of them are personal snapshots supplied to us courtesy of the person being profiled. Many are very old, one-of-a-kind photos. Most are not professional photographs, nor were they intended to be. The publisher felt that the personal nature of the stories in this book would only be enhanced by real-life, family-album-type photos, and chose to include many interesting snapshots, even if they were not quite the best quality. p.13, p.17, p.18, p.20, p.21, p.25, p.26, p.27, p.29, p.31, p.32, p.35 courtesy Tommy Nuñez; p.39, p.40, p.41, p.42, p.45, p.47, p.51, p.53 courtesy Margarita Esquiroz; p.57 Reuters/Bettmann; p.61 the Chavez Foundation; p.64, p.67, p.74 the Archives of Labor and Urban Affairs, Wayne State University; p.65, p.69, p.71, p.75 (Chris Sanchez), p.76, p.77, p.79 (Victor Alleman), p.80, p.81, p.83 (Victor Alleman) courtesy the Chavez Foundation; p.91, p.93 UPI/Bettmann.

INTRODUCTION

Kathy Escamilla

One of the fastest growing ethno-linguistic groups in the United States is a group of people who are collectively called Hispanic. The term *Hispanic* is an umbrella term which encompasses people from many nationalities, from all races, and from many social and cultural groups. The label *Hispanic* sometimes obscures the diversity of people who come from different countries and speak different varieties of Spanish. Therefore, it is crucial to know that the term *Hispanic* encompasses persons whose origins are from Spanish-speaking countries, including Spain, Mexico, Central and South America, Cuba, Puerto Rico, the Dominican Republic, and the United States. It is important also to note that Spanish is the heritage language of most Hispanics. However, Hispanics living in the United States are also linguistically diverse. Some speak mostly Spanish and little English, others are bilingual, and some speak only English.

Hispanics are often also collectively called Latinos. In addition to calling themselves Hispanics or Latinos, many people in this group also identify themselves in more specific terms according to their country of origin or their ethnic group (e.g. Cuban-American, Chicano, Puerto Rican-American, etc.) The population of Hispanics in the United States is expected to triple in the next twenty-five years, making it imperative that students in schools understand and appreciate the enormous contributions that persons of Hispanic heritage have made in the Western Hemisphere in general and in the United States in particular.

There are many who believe that in order to be successful in the United States now and in the twenty-first century, all persons from diverse cultural backgrounds, such as Hispanics, should be assimilated. To be assimilated means losing one's distinct cultural and linguistic heritage and changing to or adopting the cultural attributes of the dominant culture.

Others disagree with the assimilationist viewpoint and believe that it is both possible and desirable for persons from diverse cultural backgrounds to maintain their cultural heritage and to also contribute positively and successfully to the dominant culture. This viewpoint is called cultural pluralism, and it is from the perspective of cultural pluralism that these biographies are written. They represent persons who identify strongly with their Hispanic heritage, and who are at the same time proud of being citizens of the United States and successful contributors to U.S. society.

The biographies in these books represent the diversity of the Hispanic heritage in the United States. Persons featured are contemporary figures whose national origins range from Argentina to Arizona and whose careers and contributions cover every aspect of contemporary life in the United States. These biographies include writers, musicians, actors, journalists, astronauts, businessmen, judges, political activists, and politicians. Further, they include Hispanic women and men, and thus characterize the changing role of all women in the United States. Each person profiled in this book is a positive role model, not only for persons of Hispanic heritage, but for any person.

Collectively, these biographies demonstrate the value of cultural pluralism and a view that the future strength of the United States lies in nurturing the diversity of its human potential, not in its uniformity.

Dr. Kathy Escamilla is currently Vice President of the National Association for Bilingual Education and an Associate Professor of Bilingual Education and Multicultural Education at the University of Colorado, Denver. She previously taught at the University of Arizona, and was the Director of Bilingual Education for the Tucson Unified School District in Tucson, Arizona. Dr. Escamilla earned a B.A. degree in Spanish and Literature from the University of Colorado in 1971. Her master's degree is in bilingual education from the University of Kansas, and she earned her doctorate in bilingual education from UCLA in 1987.

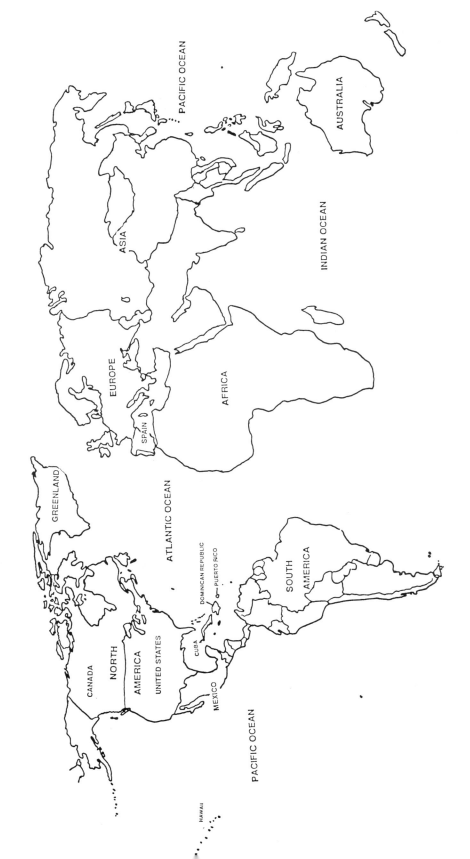

MAP OF THE WORLD

7

TOMMY NUÑEZ

NBA Referee

1939-

"Dream a little, set goals, stay in school, and take your best shot. You can make the right choices, even if you weren't born rich. If I can make it in life, so can you.**"**

Tommy Nuñez, as told to Barbara Marvis, April 1995

BIO HIGHLIGHTS

- Born September 10, 1939, Santa Maria, California; mother: Chonita Oviedo; father: Joseph Nuñez
- Grew up in poverty in government housing projects around Phoenix, Arizona
- Expelled from school numerous times; kicked out of St. Mary's High School
- Kicked out of Boys' Club for life at age thirteen
- Got in trouble with the law and was told to join Marines at age seventeen
- Earned GED in Marines and turned life around
- Married Mary Ann Solarez July 21, 1956
- GED enabled him to get job at Western Electric, 1958-1973
- Became NBA referee in 1973 (to present)
- Began community service, motivational speaking, and dropout prevention in 1978

"Just because you were not born rich does not mean you must fail," Tommy says.

TOMMY NUÑEZ

Tommy Nuñez travels from city to city each week to officiate professional basketball games for the National Basketball Association (NBA). He is one of only fifty-four NBA referees nationwide. What's more, he is the only Hispanic to officiate for any of the major league sports. But this is not what makes Tommy Nuñez the most proud. This is not what makes him so special. It is not even what he wants to be remembered for. Each year, Tommy speaks to thousands of young adults all across the nation. He gives talks in schools, in prisons, and in summer camps. Calling himself blessed with "the gift of gab," this vibrant speaker shares his life's experiences with economically disadvantaged youths, socially disadvantaged children, academically at-risk students, nonachievers and class clowns, the latchkey kids, and children who are sometimes forgotten. The faces change; the cities are different; but Tommy's message is always the same: "Stay in school," Tommy says. "You can make the right choices. You do not have to do drugs. You do not have to join gangs. Just because you were not born rich does not mean you must fail. You have a right to succeed in life. You are guaranteed the right to anything you want to achieve. But your education is your key. Whether you are rich or poor, white, black, or brown, you have access to a good education. With a good education, you can be anything you want to in life."

And just why would any of these kids listen to Tommy Nuñez, a successful NBA referee? How could Tommy know about their poverty, the welfare, the broken homes, the bad neighborhoods, the gangs, the drugs, and living a rough life? "I've been there," says Tommy. "That's where I came from. If I can make it in life, so can you." From the Phoenix barrio to the NBA, Tommy Nuñez has been there. But Tommy is special. He believes in giving back to the community he came from. He not only shares his good fortune with the less fortunate, but he shares his personal life story with kids to whom life has not always seemed fair. And he speaks from the heart. Tommy tells them how to play the cards they've been dealt.

Thomas Leonard Nuñez was born on September 10, 1939, in Santa Maria, California. He was the second of four children born to Joseph and Chonita Oviedo Nuñez. He has an older brother, Joey, and two younger sisters, Theresa and Lollie. He also has two half brothers, Steve and Timmy Nealis, from his mother's second marriage to Seymour (Steve) Nealis.

Though both of his parents were born in the United States, Tommy can trace his roots back to both Spain and Mexico. On his mother's side,

▼▼▼▼▼

From the Phoenix barrio to the NBA, Tommy Nuñez has been there.

▲▲▲▲▲▲

Though he grew up poor, he never really knew the difference until he was in his teens.

TOMMY NUÑEZ

his grandfather, Tata Oviedo, was born in Spain. Big Nana, his grandmother, was born in Mexico. On his father's side, his great-grandparents were born in Mexico. His father's parents were born in the United States.

Tommy's mother, Chonita, was always called "Toni" by her friends. Tommy remembers her as an outgoing, social person. She was born and raised near Phoenix, Arizona and had seven brothers and sisters.

Tommy's father, Joseph, was also born in Arizona. He had five brothers and one sister. Joseph and Chonita were married in 1933, when Joseph was sixteen and Toni was fourteen. The couple settled for a while in Santa Maria, California, where both Joey, Jr., and Tommy were born. Tommy's father worked for the Coca-Cola Bottling Company and in construction, cleaning windows. But Toni had asthma and the climate in California was difficult for her. The family returned to the Phoenix area when Tommy was only five.

Tommy remembers that both of his parents worked very hard when he was a youngster. Both sets of grandparents lived nearby, and he remembers one big, happy, extended family. His grandparents would watch him and his siblings while their parents worked. He had lots of cousins and friends to play with. Though he grew up poor, he never really knew the difference until he was in his teens.

Tommy was enrolled at Garfield School in 1944. His first few years were uneventful, though his parents never stressed to him the importance of an education. Tommy never took school seriously and he eventually started getting in trouble. He enjoyed talking back to the teachers. He was a smart aleck and often disrupted class. Because he and his parents moved so much, Tommy attended three different primary schools. He attended Garfield School until 1947. He attended Monroe School for fourth and fifth grades, until 1949; and he spent sixth, seventh, and eighth grades at Edison School.

Tommy, center, at about eleven years old, with friends Moises Moya on left and Alfred Arvizu on right

Tommy hung around with neighborhood kids who also weren't interested in school. By the time he was in sixth grade, his family had moved to the Dupa Villa Housing Project in East Phoenix, which was a very poor part of town. Tommy was constantly fighting in school, and he

TOMMY NUÑEZ

was often expelled for his behavior. "We used to be criticizing everybody's mama," says Tommy, "long before it was fashionable. I'd yell, 'Your mama wears combat boots' to someone loud enough and long enough for him to go ballistic on me. Next thing I'd know, someone was punching me, and of course I had to defend myself. I'd fight all day long. The teachers would get sick of this and send me to the principal. My mother would have to come bring me home. But she never said anything to me about my behavior. If she had even grounded me just once for getting in trouble, it might have sunk in, but she never did."

Although he was arrogant and had a smart mouth, Tommy was not stupid. "I made B's and C's," says Tommy, "without ever trying. I never did any homework, I think out of defiance, and I paid no attention in school. But I never failed anything. Can you imagine what I could have done had I been interested in school and done my work?"

Things got worse for Tommy as he grew older. His parents' marriage had never been good. They were always fighting, and soon the marriage broke up. His parents divorced when Tommy was eleven and in sixth grade. His father moved back to Santa Maria, California, and though Tommy did get to see him, it was only occasion-

Tommy's
only interest
in school
was sports.

ally, usually in the summer. Tommy's mother remarried several years later, but Tommy never really felt a part of his mother's life after that. Over the years, Toni married several times, and this instability contributed to the confusion that was part of Tommy's everyday life. As a result, he went to live with his grandparents most of the time. His grandmother Nuñez was always good to him and he hung out at her house anytime he wanted. He loved the way she made Cream of Wheat cereal with no lumps! Big Nana and Tata Oviedo also lived nearby, and Tommy frequently stayed with them, too. His sister Lollie went off to live with an aunt. The children were always with part of the family, but they were no longer all together under one roof.

Besides fighting, Tommy's only interest in school was sports. He played baseball, basketball, and football. His greatest motivation to stay in school was to play sports. St. Mary's High School, a private school in Phoenix, not only had a great academic reputation, but it also had a wonderful athletic reputation. Tommy would have given anything to be able to play sports for St. Mary's. His cousin Johnny Nuñez had attended St. Mary's and was an honor student. Several other cousins were at St. Mary's doing very well. One day, Tommy was given the opportunity to attend this prestigious private school. St. Mary's gave

▼▼▼▼▼▼

Tommy would have given anything to be able to play sports for St. Mary's.

▲▲▲▲▲▲

15

him a full scholarship and Tommy could not believe his luck. Attending St. Mary's meant the world to him.

"I knew I was very lucky to get the chance to go to St. Mary's," says Tommy, "but I still did not straighten up. I was just an innercity kid trying to survive. No one put any priority on my education. We did not speak about school at home. We didn't talk about homework or world events or civic responsibility. My parents were not very scholarly or educated, and they were mostly concerned about paying rent and feeding the family. There was nothing in my lifestyle that made me understand there was anything better than what I knew."

The Boys' Club of America occupied a lot of Tommy's time when he was growing up. He was kicked out for life, however, when he was only thirteen. Certainly Tommy was very mischievous, but what could he possibly have done to get kicked out – for life? "Seven of us went to the rodeo for the Boys' Club to clean up after the rodeo was over," says Tommy. "The Boys' Club would get a donation and we'd get a few bucks for our effort. Well, the soda machines still had syrup in them and the popcorn machine still had crumbs, and pretty soon we all started drinking the syrup and eating popcorn crumbs. Next thing I knew, we started throwing the crumbs at each

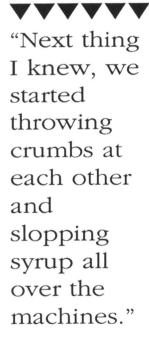

"Next thing I knew, we started throwing crumbs at each other and slopping syrup all over the machines."

other and slopping the syrup all over the machines. We ended up doing a lot of damage. We made it a bigger mess than what we were being paid to clean up! But that wasn't the end. My friends elected me to be the spokesman and said I should go ask for our five dollars' pay, despite all the destruction we had caused. Well, that was the last straw. The guy goes ballistic on me and tells me I'm out of the Boys' Club – forever!"

None of the consequences stopped any of Tommy's mischievous ways. He drove his uncle's car before he had a license. And when he was fourteen or fifteen, he and some friends swiped the wine at St. Mark's Church one Sunday; when the priest went to retrieve the wine for mass that day, there was none!

Tommy, in center sitting down, with the Boys' Club

Back at St. Mary's, Tommy was still a discipline problem. His teachers complained he was a class clown and that he did not follow the rules. He talked back, and he was constantly fighting. He was expelled several times, but he was always allowed to return. Then one day he went too far. Tommy was to play in a baseball game for St. Mary's one afternoon. He played varsity shortstop. His mother and father were never able to come see him play. But this day was going to be different. Tommy's father was coming from California to watch his game. This meant an awful lot to Tommy and he was looking forward to it. But earlier in the afternoon Tommy got in trouble with Father Brian. As punishment, Father Brian told Tommy he could not play in the ball game. Tommy was crushed. He did not know what to do. He just had to play. So Tommy played anyway and didn't say anything to anyone. He just ignored Father Brian's punishment.

Tommy is number 12 on the St. Mary's football team. He is shown fifth from the left, up front.

At the end of the game, Father Brian realized that Tommy had disobeyed him. "Why did you play when I told you not to?" asked Father Brian. Tommy did not tell Father Brian that his father was at that game – the first game he had ever seen Tommy play. He did not feel he owed anyone an explanation. And he didn't want anyone to think he was a wimp. So he did not answer – and he was expelled, permanently this time. It was just ten days before the end of his sophomore year. He didn't receive credit for the entire last semester.

The following year, 1954, Tommy enrolled at Phoenix Union High School. Though Tommy barely lasted an entire year at Phoenix Union, one very good thing did happen when he transferred schools. He met a lovely young lady named Mary Ann Solarez, who was an honor student at Phoenix. They were both fifteen years old when they met and they were also both involved with the Catholic Youth Organization at St. Mark's Church. Tommy spent a lot of time with Mary Ann over the next several years. Her family accepted him right away, and he felt very comfortable with her parents. He envied the fact that she had a very stable, two-parent home. Her father came home from work each evening and the family ate dinner together. Tommy could see right away that he wanted to be a part of a family like this.

Despite his association with Mary Ann, it was not very long before Tommy was in trouble again – this time with the law. He says he started drinking and acting stupid. He had received four traffic tickets within one month.

One day when Tommy was acting particularly stupid, he borrowed his Uncle Joe's car and went out cruising. It was in the middle of the day, and he felt he had nothing better to do. He turned a corner, not far from his home, and did not look very carefully. He sideswiped a parked car, pretended he was going to stop, but then noticed there was someone sitting in the car. He decided to keep on going. The woman in the car got his license number, and the police were wait-

▼▼▼▼▼

. . . It was not very long before Tommy was in trouble again – this time with the law.

▲▲▲▲▲

ing for him by the time he returned to Uncle Joe's house. He was taken down to the police station and turned over to a probation officer. His probation officer gave him an ultimatum: "You can join the Marines or go to jail." At that time, the Marines were often used as a place for wayward youth.

Tommy in the Marines

Just ten days after his seventeenth birthday, Tommy joined the United States Marines. His uncle Gus Oviedo had to sign for him because his mother wouldn't. She was too mad at him for all the trouble he had been getting into. His friend Kido Valenzuela joined with him to keep him company. The twosome rode a bus to San Diego for adventure in the Marines. Tommy figured he might end up like John Wayne. Not a chance.

As Kido and Tommy got off the bus in San Diego, a Marine officer was yelling and screaming at them. They started laughing, and next thing they knew they were doing push-ups all through the night. It did not take Tommy long in the Marines to learn about respect. The punishment for disrespect was so severe, being a smart aleck was no longer any fun for Tommy. He spent twelve weeks in San Diego and then ended up in the infantry, training at

Camp Pendleton; he was later shipped overseas. But his three years in the service taught him more than he had ever learned anywhere else. "The Marines really turned my life around," recalls Tommy. "I learned to be responsible for my actions, I learned about self-esteem and self-respect. I learned how to get along with others and how to control my temper. The Marines made *discipline* a meaningful word in my life."

While Tommy was in the Marines, he continued his relationship with Mary Ann. One year after he joined the Marines and one year before Mary Ann graduated from high school, Tommy and Mary Ann were married.

Tommy's platoon in the U.S. Marine Corps

It was also in the Marines that Tommy earned his GED (Graduate Equivalency Diploma). But Tommy says he still didn't know the value of his high school diploma. He was stationed in Okinawa when someone came around and asked if anyone wanted to earn his GED. Since Tommy had no orders at the time, he figured he'd go take the test. It was a cinch for him. But, he never realized the importance of that degree until he was out of the Marines. Then he got his first job in 1958 with Western Electric, where he was trained to be a switchboard repairman. By now he had a wife to support, and the job at Western Electric was only available to those with a high school degree. Tommy worked for Western Electric (then part of AT&T) for fifteen years in various capacities.

Tommy and Mary Ann had two sons — Tommy Jr., born in 1959; and Donnie, born in 1961 — and a daughter, Colleen, born in 1962. Tommy and Mary Ann set out to provide a different home life for their children from the one Tommy had known and more like the one Mary Ann had known. Tommy and Mary Ann did stress the importance of education to all of their children. Tommy and Mary Ann watched out for each of their children and disciplined them well. "If my children ever got out of line," says Tommy, "they were grounded. We let them know we cared about them and we cared how they behaved. We were always there for them. I have to give Mary Ann most of the credit for the good job she did with the kids, because she was around much more than I was. In later years, she was able to stay at home with the kids, and this made a positive impact on their lives. We never had any trouble with any of our kids, and they all ended up doing very well in school, including Debbie, my niece, whom Mary Ann and I adopted when she was thirteen."

Tommy's involvement with the local games gave him a new perspective on life. He enjoyed officiating, and he was good at it.

TOMMY NUÑEZ

As a young man, Tommy played some semipro baseball and fast-pitch softball for a few years. He was also interested in the local high school sports. His cousin Johnny officiated for the Arizona State Interscholastic Association, which governed all high school sports. Through Johnny, Tommy got involved with the local high school games. He signed up to officiate high school football, basketball, and baseball on the freshman and junior varsity levels to make some extra money for his growing family. He also officiated at the city leagues, at the parks and recreation leagues, and at the YMCA.

Tommy's involvement with the local games gave him a new perspective on life. He enjoyed officiating, and he was good at it. He liked the people involved with the local sports, and he liked working at something that was as organized as the high school and league sports. It had a great impact on his self-esteem. He enjoyed the respect he was shown as a referee, and he liked the people with whom he was associated. They made him feel good about himself. They made him feel special. Because he had felt he had been a nobody all his life, this association made him feel like he was somebody. And it was a great feeling.

Tommy continued to work hard to provide a decent lifestyle for his family. He refereed

Tommy Nuñez

some junior college games, but the only four-year college games he ever officiated were for Grand Canyon University.

In 1966 the Phoenix Suns had just become a new franchise. Tommy met two people who were associated with the Suns and who would eventually change his life. Ted Podleski had been an American Legion baseball coach before going to work for the Phoenix Suns. (Ted is now director of the Arizona Osteopathic Association.) Bob Machen had officiated high school sports with Tommy for several years. He eventually became a ticket manager for the Suns. (Bob Machen is now the director of the America West Arena, where the Phoenix Suns play.) One day in 1970, the Suns had a summer rookie game, and Ted and Bob asked Tommy to officiate the game. Tommy thought this might be fun so he said, "Sure."

When Ted and Bob saw Tommy at the rookie game, they thought he had potential. They asked him if he had ever thought of trying out at the NBA referee camp in New York. Tommy hadn't. Officiating major league sports was way beyond anything he had ever dreamed about. Ted encouraged him to give it a try. But Tommy was overwhelmed. "At the time, I was too afraid I'd fail," recalls Tommy. "I didn't really give it any serious thought. Here I was at thirty years old,

Were they surprised when they found out he was chosen as one of five finalists from many hundreds of applicants!

and I'd never even been on an airplane. I'd never been east of Globe, Arizona, and these guys were talking about going to New York to try out for the big leagues. I said, 'No way!'"

In 1971 Tommy got another chance to referee a summer rookie game for the Suns. Here he met an NBA referee named Darell Garretson (now supervisor of all the NBA referees), who also mentioned to Tommy that he thought he had potential. Ted Podleski, Bob Machen, and Darell put together some letters of recommendation. Darell spoke to Mendy Rudolph, who was chief of staff at the time, and Tommy was invited to go to Buffalo, New York, in 1972 to try out for the NBA referee staff. By now he had had some time to think about the

Tommy talks to Darell Garretson at his first season game, Phoenix vs. Detroit, on December 13, 1973.

opportunity, and he figured he really didn't have much to lose by trying out. After all, he had a steady job, and he really didn't need another one. So Tommy traveled to New York. (His friends were all sure he'd be right back.) Were they surprised when they found out that he was chosen as one of five finalists from many hundreds of applicants! The five finalists went to referee camp with the other permanent referees that summer of 1972. Tommy got the opportunity to officiate five preseason games. He remembers that first preseason game as if it were yesterday.

The game was Chicago at Portland in October 1972 and Tommy was working with Jake O'Donnell. "I was horrendous," Tommy remembers. "I hardly blew my whistle at all, maybe only four or five times in the first half. I was probably wrong every time. I couldn't get the jump ball up high enough. The centers trapped the ball going up on the first toss. I don't think the second one ever came down. I had never worked with guys that tall in my life! Everything I'd learned, everything I'd worked for, I just forgot. It was a traumatic experience."

Tommy has to watch the players closely.

But Jake was good to him. He told Tommy that everyone was scared his first time out. "The pros are fifty times the caliber of your best college team," Jake told Tommy. "It's not easy to referee. Just calm down and relax. You'll catch on. Everyone is nervous in his first game."

By the fifth preseason game, Tommy's refereeing had improved, but he was still not confident that he had what it took to be a professional NBA referee. Others were, however. In 1973 Tommy was offered his first contract with the

NBA referees. John Nucatola hired him and was his first supervisor. Mendy Rudolph was also behind Tommy. John and Mendy believed in Tommy. They encouraged him to continue and taught him a lot about officiating basketball.

"To be a successful referee," says Tommy, "you can't worry about being popular. You do need to have a reputation for being fair. The official's primary function is to call things that give a player an unfair advantage. We're like highway patrolmen. We don't catch all the speeders, but we get enough to keep the game under control. Pro basketball is the hardest of all the sports to officiate. Things happen very fast."

Tommy on left, with NBA referees Woody Mayfield and Hue Hollins

Tommy travels every week, wherever he is asked to go. He visits all the NBA cities several times each year. He has taken Mary Ann with him on some of his trips. He never knows exactly where he'll be next. And there are no excused absences. Tommy remembers working when he had the flu. "The only reason you could be absent," he says, "is if your mortician calls." Each referee must work very hard at every game. In between games, they have to work out to keep in shape.

"We're not allowed to associate with the players," says Tommy.

TOMMY NUÑEZ

"We're not allowed to associate with the players, either," says Tommy. "We can't travel on the same plane or eat in the same restaurant at the same time. We must be totally impartial. There are NBA observers at nearly every game, who watch every move you make. The whole game is filmed and sent back to New York, where each ref is evaluated every season. And keep in mind that wherever we go, we're always the visitors. We have no home court."

As time went on, Tommy became very comfortable on the court. As he got more experience, he became a good referee. His job allowed him to give his family things that he never had growing up. This made Tommy proud. One day, he decided he should give something back. "I didn't dream this career," says Tommy. "I didn't plan it. I didn't even work toward it. I was just lucky and it found me. But since I have had such good fortune in my life, I really wanted to give something back to the community I came from." So, beginning in 1978, Tommy Nuñez began community work in his off-season. All of his work has been for kids.

As a summer hobby in 1978 and 1979, Tommy worked as a youth counselor for Chicanos Por La Causa, a summer youth training and employment program. In this program, about 130 students between the ages of fourteen and twenty-one worked on neighborhood beautification, had the opportunity to acquire work experience, and had many recreational activities during the six-week period. Tommy and codirector Ruben Calderon helped the young adults accomplish a great deal in those two summers. They helped refurbish several homes in their neighborhoods and cleaned garbage and debris from vacant lots. They renovated Cana Hall, owned by Sacred Heart Church, in exchange for rent-free use of the auditorium for recreation, lunches, and rap sessions. The workers were paid minimum wage and had to qualify on the basis of financial need. "We tell these kids the good things and the bad things," Tommy said at the time. "We want them to become productive citizens, and we do it by showing them a little bit of love. We try to instill self-respect, pride, and responsibility." Tommy was able to share his experiences with

Tommy with Charles Barkley of the Phoenix Suns.

The kids liked listening to Tommy because he shared the same background with them.

these young adults. He told them what he had learned. He thought he had some motivational messages to share. And he was right. The program was a big success. The kids cooperated with one another and hardly anyone was ever absent. The kids liked listening to Tommy because he shared the same background with them. He knew what it was like to grow up disadvantaged. Tommy liked working with these kids so much, he thought he would like to work with children as a career. So he expanded his efforts.

In 1980, Tommy was hired by the Arizona Department of Economic Security for their Job Training Partnership Administration Programs, which he does in the summer in the basketball off-season. He has worked at this job every summer to the present. The summer youth employment and training program works with socially and economically disadvantaged youths, aged fourteen to twenty-one, who are in school or who have dropped out. The program encourages these young adults to stay in school or to drop back in. It encourages the kids to learn about the world of work, gives them a chance to raise their self-image, a chance for some on-the-job-training, and a chance to earn some money. Tommy was hired to monitor the program for the state. He visits all the work sites and makes sure everything is in compliance with all laws. He is also a keynote speaker at most of the conferences for the participants.

Tommy does not completely forget about basketball every summer. He has donated his time over the years to referee for many charitable games, from Magic Johnson's Summer All-Star Basketball Classic, which benefits the United Negro College Fund, to giving a Youth Basketball Clinic to benefit Chicanos Por La Causa. He puts together three-day, free basketball/stay-in-school camps and gets NBA players to volunteer to spend a day with the kids. Some of these basketball camps have been held in Yakima, Washington; West Sacramento, California; Woodland, California; Houston, Texas; and around Phoenix. In Stanfield, Arizona, Tommy raises money to sponsor migrant children to go to Disneyland and to buy them clothes and food. But the highlight of Tommy's summer comes on Labor Day weekend, when he hosts the Tommy Nuñez National Hispanic Basketball Classic. The tournament raises funds for academic and athletic activities for disadvantaged youth. Over the years, the event has grown from eight teams participating in 1981 to more than thirty teams in 1994. The teams are composed of volunteer adult players. Tommy officiates the games along with thirteen other NBA referees, who also donate their time. Every other year, thirty refer-

Tommy and his wife, Mary Ann

TOMMY NUÑEZ

ees come from Spain! Many of the games are played at St. Mary's High School (yes, the same high school Tommy was kicked out of; today St. Mary's calls Tommy Nuñez the biggest celebrity

Tommy and friends, taken at Colleen's wedding. From left to right, top to bottom: Kino Flores, José Muñoz, Earl Wilcox, Rudy Santa Cruz, Frank Hidalgo, Henry Peralta, Sal Martinez, Ray Aguilar, Victor Flores, Nick Rios, Tommy, and Ruben Calderon

they ever kicked out!). Tommy raises funds without charging admission to the games. He gets sponsors such as Coca-Cola; Nestlé; Budweiser; Bank One; Phoenix Newspapers, Inc.; Phoenix Greyhound Park; and Sportsmans Park of Chicago, Illinois to donate funds. And he raises money from concession sales and team entry fees. In 1994 he raised $12,000 in four days, which was used to create two-year community college scholarships for local students.

Tommy has also worked for the Arizona Department of Education. In the early 1990's he visited many schools, giving talks to at-risk students. He gave a seminar called "Take Your Best Shot!" In his seminar, Tommy stressed the importance of staying in school, taking care of oneself, and saying yes to life.

Tommy tells all young adults that they can succeed at anything. They can aspire to any job they want in life. "Be the best you can be for yourself," he says. "You don't have to be a Rhodes scholar, but you do need a high school education. You can go on to college, if you want to. It's okay to have any honorable job, but if you want to be the boss, you should strive for that, too. Unless your parents have money or you hit the lottery, you'll have to be prepared to earn your own way. You can't do that without a good education."

Tommy taught these very same lessons to his own children. Each one graduated from St. Mary's High School, with honors. Father Blaise from St. Mary's once remarked, "There is a God in Heaven, Tommy! Your kids are a miracle!"

Tommy's children are all grown now. In fact, he has eleven grandchildren. His oldest son, Tommy, Jr., is a teacher at – you guessed it – St. Mary's High School. He is their head baseball coach and he is a college basketball referee. He

▼▼▼▼▼▼
Tommy's children are all grown now. In fact, he has eleven grand-children.
▲▲▲▲▲▲

TOMMY NUÑEZ

and his wife, Joanie, have twin boys, Alex and Michael, and a daughter, Kaitlyn. Tommy's second son, Donnie, is a supervisor for the Job Training Partnership Administration in the School and Summer Youth Training and Employment program for Maricopa County. (Maricopa County includes the towns all around Phoenix, Arizona, commonly referred to as "the Valley.") This is the same program that Tommy monitors for the state of Arizona every summer. Donnie also referees high school and junior college basketball games. Donnie and his wife, Cathy, have two daughters, Carissa and Brianna. Colleen has previously worked for State Farm Insurance Company, but in 1995 was taking time off to be with her children. She and her husband, Bob, have three children: David, Jay James, and Brigette. Debbie, a bilingual teacher's aide for the Phoenix Elementary School District, is married to Freddie Santiago. They have three children: Monique, Vanessa, and Shana (Azusena).

In 1994 Tommy was honored by the Hispanic Heritage Awards for excellence in sports. The nation's leading Hispanic organizations nominate people for the awards, and they all gathered at a celebration for Tommy and several other recipients on September 19 at the National Building Museum in Washington, D.C. Since Tommy's work is all about kids, he decided to take one of

Tommy says he'll never forget where he came from.

them to the awards ceremony with him. Pedro (Pete) Posado, then a Carl Hayden High School senior, won the trip when he entered an essay contest at school. Pete accompanied Tommy to the ceremony and introduced him. It was the first time Pete had ever been on a plane. Tommy said, "I could have taken anyone I wanted with me, maybe one of the NBA players, but that's not what I'm about. I want to help the kids, so it meant more to me that one of them accompany me to Washington."

Tommy and Mary Ann with their eleven grandchildren. From top to bottom: Michael, Carissa, Asuzena, Brianna, Jay, David, Kaitlyn, Alex, Brigette, Monique, and Vanessa

Tommy says he'll never forget where he came from. He chooses to remember all the hard times growing up. It's what motivates him to help others. Today, Tommy Nuñez, who was never on a plane before he was thirty, has flown all over the world. He is a living example that the American dream is alive and well. Tommy knows you can be anything you want to be in America, if you work hard enough.

MARGARITA ESQUIROZ

Lawyer, Judge
1945-

"My advice to young adults who would like to have a career in law is just this: Work very hard, study hard, and stay focused. Excel as much as you can in school. Discipline yourself to study as much as you can and become the best [person] you can possibly become. Be honest and have a good reputation, because that's really all you have. That will open new doors. **"**

Judge Margarita Esquiroz, as told to Barbara Marvis, May 1995

BIO HIGHLIGHTS

- Born February 7, 1945, Havana, Cuba; mother: Luisa (Martinez); father: Mario Esquiroz
- Attended exclusive all-girls private Catholic school, Merici Academy in Cuba; school closed by the government in April 1962, before the end of her junior year
- Left Cuba in April 1962 on a visa waiver; finished high school in the United States through correspondence course from La Salle Extension University in Chicago, Illinois
- Earned A.A. degree from Miami-Dade Community College, 1969; Bachelor's degree in Business Administration from University of Miami, 1971; and Juris Doctor from University of Miami Law School, 1974
- Worked as legal secretary to attorney Robert Lewison, 1965-1968
- Assistant Attorney General for State of Florida, 1974-1979
- Appointed Judge of Industrial Claims by Governor Bob Graham in 1979; first Hispanic female judge appointed in Florida
- Appointed Circuit Judge of the eleventh judicial district in Dade County, 1984; elected to the position later that year

In 1979, Margarita Esquiroz became the first Hispanic female to be appointed a judge in the state of Florida.

MARGARITA ESQUIROZ

In 1979, Margarita Esquiroz became the first Hispanic female to be appointed a judge in the state of Florida. This fact becomes even more incredible when you know that Margarita was a refugee who fled Castro's Cuba in 1962, armed with only a brief course in shorthand and typing. For the first several years after she arrived in the United States, she worked in various secretarial positions, while working her way through school. Her rise to judgeship occurred only five years after she became a U.S. citizen on July 4, 1974.

Margarita Esquiroz was born in Havana, Cuba on February 7, 1945. She was the second of two children born to Luisa Martinez and Mario Esquiroz. She has an older sister, Luisa, born in 1938.

The Esquiroz family enjoyed a comfortable lifestyle in Cuba. Margarita's father, born in 1907, was an architect. He designed houses and housing developments. He also owned a bank that provided financing for building houses. He had a lot of private-business contracts and some government contracts. His business provided the family with all the amenities. Margarita's mother, born in 1914, was a homemaker.

From the time she was five years old, Margarita attended Merici Academy, an exclusive private girls' school run by Ursuline nuns. This was an American school, and most of the nuns were either American, Canadian, or British. Margarita was taught English from the day she entered school. In elementary school, the entire morning was taught in English. The afternoon was taught in Spanish. By the time she got to secondary school, her entire day, except for one period, was taught in English. She also learned French and Latin. "And, of course," says Margarita, "there was religion all over the place."

Margarita studied classical ballet, piano, and guitar. Three or four times every week, she had ballet lessons, which she enjoyed very much. She never considered a career as a dancer, however. She grew up believing that one could not make a very good living in the arts, and her talents and major interests weren't in professional ballet. Margarita was more inclined to study, and she felt she could "be somebody" with her exclusive education.

An early picture of Margarita, taken in Cuba

In 1959, it appeared as though the comfortable lifestyle that the Esquiroz family had come to know would soon cease to exist. In that year, Fidel Castro and a band of rebels overthrew the Cuban dictator, Fulgencio Batista, who had controlled Cuba since the 1930's (except for a period of time after World War II). Castro set up a

MARGARITA ESQUIROZ

Margarita studied piano as a young girl growing up in Cuba.

socialist government and named himself president. His government allowed only one political party, the Cuban Communist Party. He then set out to end all free enterprise on the island. He declared that no private businesses could exist. They all would belong to the government. Castro began to take over the sugar mills and all the other businesses.

Between 1960 and 1961, thousands of people left the island. Those who owned businesses or believed in free enterprise were among the first to flee. Many came to the United States. Some went to Mexico and Spain. Most of Margarita's friends and family left the island during this time. "We stayed in Cuba for three and a half years after the revolution," Margarita says. "I was the last of my group of friends to leave. Most of the nuns at my school left, and we were being taught by lay teachers. The people with the best opportunities, the best education . . . these were the people who left first and settled around Miami." In 1961 the United States ended diplomatic relations with Cuba.

In 1962 things got even worse as Castro grew more powerful. "I was in school one day," Margarita recalls, "when I saw them walk in. Men in green uniforms came in and took over the school. Actually, it was a combination of the government taking over the school and the religious people fleeing the country. The nuns left, the priests left. All the schools as we knew them, the schools where the middle and upperclass [children] received their education, just didn't exist after 1962." In April, just a few months before the end of Margarita's junior year, Merici Academy was closed. However, the students were given certificates of completion, saying they had finished the year.

Margarita, at about six years old, in front of her house in Cuba

Then the government came and took her father's business. "They took his bank and they confiscated his bank account," says Margarita. "The government would not allow any enterprise that made a profit. The schools couldn't operate privately. The government took over everything."

Eventually, the Esquiroz family faced the reality of their situation. They, too, had to leave. "It was a combination of the reality of what was happening combined with a lot of panic," recalls Margarita. Her parents sent her and her sister to the United States. They joined some aunts and uncles who had already settled in Miami. "Luisa and I got out on visa waivers that were issued to students," remembers Margarita. "We didn't know when our parents would join us. It could have been six months, a year, or maybe never." Luckily, her parents were able to get out of Cuba just three weeks later, and the whole family was reunited in Miami. All of her relatives had left Cuba by that time.

Margarita (center) celebrated her birthday every year with a costume party. Her birthday falls around carnival time in Havana.

Now everyone had to think about making a new life in a strange land. This was easier for the younger people than for their parents, aunts, and uncles. Luisa, Margarita, and their friends all spoke English, but most of the older generation did not. Still, Margarita tells us, this was a bad age for all of this to happen. "It disrupts your whole life," she says. "This is the time when you are supposed to be thinking about what you want to do in life. You start making plans for the future, and this was a very large disruption."

Margarita's first challenge when she got to the United States was to finish her high school education. She needed only four courses to get her diploma. She took the courses she needed by mail from La Salle Extension University in Chicago, Illinois. She also needed to get a job to help support of the family, who had left Cuba with nothing. "Here one has to produce," says Margarita. "It's not a matter of knowing art and literature. You have to earn your keep through something useful and practical."

Her father found a job with an architectural firm, at a salary. He was never able to pass his architectural boards in the United States, and he never again owned his own business. Though he was able to support his family on his salary, the challenge and satisfaction of owning a business eluded him here.

Margarita had taken a brief course in typing and shorthand before she left Cuba, and she used these skills to find employment in Miami. She worked for a short time as a secretary for an exile student organization and then as a medical secretary. In February 1965, she took a job with Miami attorney Robert Lewison as his legal secretary, while she continued her schooling. She gained valuable experience working in his law office. She worked for Lewison until December 1968.

After she earned her high school diploma, she enrolled at Miami-Dade Community College and took courses at night. In December 1969, she was awarded an associate in arts degree with a 4.0 cumulative average. She not only graduated with honors and on the dean's list, but she was the recipient of an honor scholarship. She used

"Luisa and I got out on visa waivers that were issued to students," remembers Margarita.

this scholarship to continue her education at the University of Miami, where she earned a bachelor's degree in business administration in 1971. She originally thought she might have a career in accounting.

"I was disappointed to find [accounting] didn't suit me. When I graduated, I didn't feel satisfied, happy, or psyched up about my career. The human element was missing. It is a dry profession," says Margarita.

She decided her career should be more people-oriented. In her senior year at the University of Miami, Margarita had worked in the Law Library. That, combined with her previous experience of being a legal secretary, led her to believe that she would enjoy a career in law. She saw this as an opportunity to work closely with people and as an intellectual challenge. So she enrolled at the University of Miami Law School, where she was awarded her Juris Doctor degree in 1974. She graduated cum laude and was ranked in the top 10 percent of her class.

Margarita initially thought about a career in private practice. She was attracted to civil litigation but changed her mind when she graduated. "I'm not a moneymaker," Margarita says, because private practice would have paid better. She decided, however, that public service was more suited to her, and in July of 1974 she accepted

"I was disappointed to find [accounting] didn't suit me. . . . The human element was missing."

a position as an assistant attorney general for the State of Florida. Margarita mostly handled appeals for the state, generally in criminal cases. She appeared in both the state appellate (appeals) courts and in the federal courts. She handled several cases in the circuit court on behalf of the state, where she defended the state against claims made by people who sought to establish with the court that they were rightful heirs to money that would have otherwise been turned over to the state. She also defended the state against challenges to the constitutionality of the state statutes at both the trial and appellate levels.

On May 24, 1979, then Florida Governor Bob Graham appointed Margarita Esquiroz to be Judge of Industrial Claims of the State of Florida. She became the first female Hispanic judge in Florida. The City of Miami Mayor and Commission then proclaimed that August 26, 1979, would be "Margarita Esquiroz's Day," in recognition of her being the first Latina judge appointed in Florida.

Margarita with her family: father Mario, mother Luisa, and sister, Luisa

MARGARITA ESQUIROZ

As Judge of Industrial Claims, the Honorable Margarita Esquiroz presided over cases that involved worker's compensation claims, where workers were injured on the job. She heard the cases and had to act as both judge and jury, while she decided significant issues dealing with the law and medical matters. Each case required that she issue a written finding of fact and a conclusion of law. Some of the cases that she heard also included compensation cases for victims of crime, filed under Florida law.

Five years later, on January 24, 1984, Governor Graham appointed Judge Esquiroz to the Eleventh Judicial District Circuit of Dade County, Florida. She became one of three Latino Circuit Court Judges of the fifty-seven Circuit Court Judges on the bench in Dade County at the time. In March 1984, she was invested by Lieutenant Governor Wayne Mixson. A crowd of more than 250 spectators and fifty robed judges attended the ceremony. Everyone applauded as her parents placed her blue robe on her shoulders. She received lots of congratulatory mail. Among the letters was a mailgram from one of her former employers. It read: "You are the first secretary I ever had who is a circuit judge. Congratulations . . . Bob Lewison." She had 1,700 civil cases waiting for her attention when she assumed her new position.

MARGARITA ESQUIROZ

Judge Esquiroz was appointed to her position by the governor because a vacancy existed before elections. Normally, Circuit Court Judges in Florida are elected, and in order to keep her position, Judge Esquiroz had to be elected later that year. Judge Esquiroz captured nearly 90 percent of the Hispanic vote, plus solid support from both Anglo and African-American voters, to retain her position for another six years.

Judge Esquiroz was assigned to the General Jurisdiction of the Court through December of 1984. She heard cases involving a wide variety of legal matters, including personal injury cases, commercial litigation, and divorce proceedings.

Chief Judge Gerald Wetherington swears in Margarita Esquiroz in March 1984.

In January 1985, Judge Esquiroz was assigned to the Criminal Division, and she presided over the trials of persons accused of committing crimes. In February 1989, Judge Esquiroz was again reassigned to the General Jurisdiction, only now cases including divorces, child custody, and support were removed from the General Jurisdiction and reassigned to the newly established

47

Family Division. She still held this position in 1995.

Today, Judge Esquiroz is one of only five Hispanics of the sixty-eight Circuit Court judges in Dade County. Three of the five Hispanic judges are female. There are another four Hispanic judges at the County Court level, one on the District Court of Appeals, and one more on the Federal Bench.

Judge Esquiroz enjoys her career as a judge; she knows she made the right career decision when she decided to go into law. "I enjoy the challenge," she says. "[I'm] never bored . . . always going. [I like] having the ability to make decisions that [I] can be completely clean about. [As a judge,] you can speak your intellect; you can make intelligent and honest decisions instead of [like a lawyer] having to argue a position that might be wrong or you might not believe in. If he [the lawyer] is going to represent a client, he has to argue his case, and [a person] can lose objectivity by getting too involved in [the] client's cause. Sometimes there is no way you can believe you are right under the law, and yet, even if you do not believe you are right, you have to advocate that [for your client].

"Every individual is entitled to his day in court and to the best representation possible. A lawyer must advance the best position for [his

"It is not pleasant to tell somebody [he] cannot have what [he] wants."

client's] cause. He must put the argument in the best way. Sometimes the cases are not so clear cut.

"The judge has to hear the evidence and then apply the law, and hopefully the truth will prevail. [I] try to reach a fair result that has balance."

Though Judge Esquiroz clearly enjoys the challenge that is presented to her daily, there are aspects of her job that are not so pleasant. "It is not pleasant to tell somebody [he] cannot have what [he] wants," she says. "When somebody comes before you, somebody wins and somebody loses. It is not pleasant, but you have to do it. It is like a doctor that has to tell somebody she has an illness; it is not pleasant, but that's the doctor's job. I'm sure doctors don't enjoy that aspect of it, they couldn't possibly. [But] it is part of what we chose to do in life, and you learn to deal with it professionally . . .

"It is also not pleasant to have to sentence somebody to jail. [I] do it out of a sense of responsibility. I don't derive any pleasure [when I have to] send somebody to jail for fifty years. But I've got to do this. It is my responsibility. I have to willingly accept that responsibility, and I do."

Judge Esquiroz tells us that she can never let her feelings get in the way of her being able to apply the law. A judge must always enforce and

"My job is to enforce whatever the law is. By and large, our laws are wise."

MARGARITA ESQUIROZ

apply the law. "We are instruments of the law," she says. "I've always had respect for the law. I've never been a rebel when it comes to [this]. My job is to enforce whatever the law is. By and large, our laws are wise, with very few exceptions. For example, it is not relevant whether a judge believes in the death penalty or not. The Supreme Court has ruled it is constitutional; therefore, if it is the law in your state, and the circumstances of the crime call for the death penalty, you must apply it."

Judge Esquiroz says that her job sometimes becomes difficult when she sees a good person charged with committing an awful crime. She often sees elements of human failing, and she remembers some particularly sad cases where a criminal act was not necessarily intentional. There was a case of a twenty-year-old girl who was charged with shaking her baby to death. "She shook a one-month-old because it was crying and the baby had to be hospitalized. It died several months later in a coma. The woman was otherwise a good citizen and came from a good family. This was a jury case and they found her guilty of third-degree murder, though she had been charged with first-degree. I think in her case, the sentence had to be three to seven years in jail with some probation. I think she was out on bond pending appeal when I left the Criminal Division, and I don't recall if the court later mitigated her sentence or not."

Cases that involve children are also particularly difficult for many judges. When the Family Division was still a part of the General Jurisdiction Division, Judge Esquiroz heard child custody cases as well. "These days we [in Florida] have shared parental responsibility where you can actually split up a kid. One parent has to be the residential parent and you've got to name one. As long as you have a competent mother, she might be the residential parent under Florida state laws; but you can give visitation to the father, so the child could actually [stay] at the father's house almost half the week. You can share the time almost equally. You don't [often] wind up doing that because of school, but weekends are a good time for the nonresidential parent to have the [children]. . . .The only time you can cut off visitation from the nonresidential parent is if that parent is doing something against the child's [best] interests . . . like a parent who uses drugs. Then you have to lecture the parents and counsel them. Being a judge in the Family Division is a little like being a social worker," Judge Esquiroz says. "Here, you're less of a jurist than any place else."

Judge Esquiroz enjoys several hobbies and has recently started taking ballet lessons again.

In 1991 Margarita Esquiroz was the recipient of the Hispanic Heritage Award for leadership.

MARGARITA ESQUIROZ

She quit her dance lessons many years ago when she came to the United States, because she needed to concentrate on her studies. Then, around 1980, she started going again, but could not organize her time well enough to continue. Now, though her career keeps her very busy and she is often still at work at seven o'clock at night, she finds she is better prepared to stick to a schedule. She attends the Martha Mahr School of Dance in Coral Gables twice a week. She also enjoys watching professional ballets and holds season tickets every year to the Miami City Ballet. She is a fan of Fernando Bujones, who is a professional dancer and now lives in Miami. She also hopes to resume her piano lessons again, soon.

Judge Esquiroz has been recognized with many awards over the years. In 1982 she received the Floridana Award, given to the ten most outstanding members of the Cuban Women's Club. She was named "Outstanding

In 1991, Judge Esquiroz was the recipient of the Hispanic Heritage Award for leadership. She is pictured here in a newspaper article along with Dr. Joseph Fernandez and Eduardo Mata, who also won awards that year. Rita Moreno presented the awards.

MARGARITA ESQUIROZ

Woman of 1984" by the Miami Ballet Society. And in 1991 Margarita Esquiroz was the recipient of the Hispanic Heritage Award for leadership. She was honored at a celebration on September 16, 1991, during Hispanic Heritage month, at the Organization of American States Building in Washington, D.C.

Margarita with family and friends. From left to right, standing: her grandmother Graziella Varela de Martinez, Carlos Villa, Margarita, her mother Luisa, her father Mario, her sister Luisa, her aunt Graciela Martinez de Peña; sitting: Blanca Rosa Villa, and Dr. and Mrs. Torres. Taken in August 1960 at her mother's birthday celebration in Vara Dero, Cuba

Her advice to young adults who would like to follow in her footsteps to a career in law is this: "Work very hard, study hard, and stay focused. Excel as much as you can in school; discipline yourself to study as much as you can and become the best [person] you can possibly become. Be honest and have a good reputation, because that is really all you have. That will open new doors."

Judge Esquiroz is a devoted jurist, and she is committed to her career. Her greatest satisfaction is "to do something really right for an individual who couldn't get justice any other way."

CESAR E. CHAVEZ

Farm Labor Leader

1927-1993

"Our movement is spreading like flames across a dry plain. The time has come for the liberation of the poor farm worker. *Viva la causa!* **"**

Cesar E. Chavez, Founder, United Farm Workers of America, 1969

BIO HIGHLIGHTS

- Born March 31, 1927, near Yuma, Arizona; mother: Juana Estrada; father: Librado Chavez
- Attended Laguna School in North Gila Valley
- 1939, Chavez farm sold for taxes; family travels through California as migrant workers
- 1944-46, served in U.S. Navy
- Married Helen Fabela, October 22, 1948
- Met Fred Ross of Community Service Organization (CSO), 1952
- 1952-1962, worked for CSO
- 1958, named general director of CSO
- 1962, organized farm labor union and held first convention
- 1965, NFWA strike against grape growers in California; boycott against Schenley
- 1966, union marches from Delano to Sacramento; settlement/ contract with Schenley
- 1968, twenty-five-day fast to stress importance of nonviolence in cause
- July 1970, five-year grape boycott ended
- 1972, Chavez fasts for twenty-four days
- 1975, Agricultural Labor Relations Act (ALRA) passed the California legislature
- 1982, political entity in California refuses to enforce ALRA
- 1984, grape boycott
- 1988, Chavez fasts for thirty-six days to protest use of pesticides on grapes
- April 23, 1993, dies in sleep

Cesar E. Chavez

Cesar Chavez was still on union business in San Luis, Arizona, when he died peacefully in his sleep on April 23, 1993. An estimated fifty thousand people followed his plain pine casket in a three-mile-long march from Memorial Park in Delano, California, to the funeral mass at the United Farm Workers' field office west of town.

For much of his life, Cesar Chavez lived penniless. He was the only national union leader in recent history who refused to wear a tie and took no salary. He devoted everything he had to the United Farm Workers, the first effective farm workers union ever created in the United States. "Without a union, the people are always cheated, and they are so innocent," said Cesar. Cesar Chavez devoted his entire life, all his energy, and every penny he earned so that migrant farm workers could earn a decent living and raise their families with dignity.

Cesar Estrada Chavez was born on March 31, 1927, near Yuma, Arizona. He was the second of six children born to Librado and Juana Estrada Chavez. He had an older sister, Rita (1925); a younger brother, Richard (1929); and two younger sisters, Helena (who died very young) and Vicky (1933). His youngest brother, Lenny, was born in 1934.

"Without a union, the people are always cheated, and they are so innocent."

Cesar E. Chavez

Cesario Chavez, Cesar's grandfather, left Chihuahua, Mexico, in the 1880's. He crossed the border into El Paso, Texas, and worked on the railroads and in the fields to make enough money to send for his wife and their fourteen children. One of his children, Librado, Cesar's father, was two years old when he came to the United States in 1888.

Grandfather Chavez settled his family on free land near Yuma, Arizona, in the North Gila Valley along the Colorado River. He started a hauling business there and homesteaded on more than one hundred acres. He started the family farm three years before Arizona even became a state. One by one, his children married and built homes of their own

nearby. The entire area was filled with relatives. Librado stayed on the farm until he was thirty-eight years old to help his father. He married Juana Estrada on June 15, 1924. She was also from Chihuahua, Mexico, and was thirty-two when she married Librado. Their first child, Rita, was born in 1925.

Members of the United Farm Workers watch over Cesar Chavez as he lays in state during a public viewing on April 28, 1993.

Grandfather Chavez settled his family on free land near Yuma, Arizona, in the North Gila Valley along the Colorado River.

CESAR E. CHAVEZ

Librado bought a business not far from the family ranch. He owned three buildings, which included a grocery store, where they lived; a service station; and a pool hall. Cesar was born in 1927, and Richard was born two years later. Librado needed more land to expand his business, so one day he made a deal with a neighboring farmer. The neighbor, an Anglo (a Mexican American term for a white man), needed some land cleared, and Librado offered to supply the back-breaking labor in exchange for some of the land. Day after day, Librado pulled stumps and thrashed weeds. After several months, when the land was all cleared, Librado requested the deed to the land he had earned. But the owner double-crossed him. He sold the land that Librado wanted to another man, Justus Jackson. Librado went straight to a lawyer, who advised him just to offer to buy the land from the new owner. Librado borrowed the money from the bank, but he was not able to pay the interest on the loan. The lawyer then bought the land from Librado and sold it back to the original owner!

During the Depression, many of Librado's customers lost their jobs. They could not pay him for what they needed from his grocery store. Librado was very generous and extended them credit so their families could eat. But soon Librado also could not pay his bills. He had to sell his grocery store to pay off his debts. To save money, he moved his family back to his mother's house, where she was now living alone since Cesario's death.

Cesar attended Laguna School in North Gila Valley. He remembered getting up very early every morning with his brother Richard to get water from the canal to give to the animals. They would gather eggs and do some other work around the farm. Then they would come in, get washed and dressed for school, and eat some breakfast. They were almost always late. They had to walk about a mile to school, and in the cold weather they did not have clothes that were warm enough. They used to run between their relatives' houses, stopping in each one along they way to get warmed up for a minute.

Cesar didn't always enjoy school. "In class, one of my biggest problems was the language," he said years later. "Of course, we bitterly resented not being able to speak Spanish, but they insisted that we learn English. They said that if we were American, then we should speak the language, and if we wanted to speak Spanish, we should go back to Mexico."

In 1936 money began to trickle back into the area, and some people were able to find jobs. Librado and a cousin were able to rent the pool

When the land was all cleared, Librado requested the deed to the land he had earned. But the owner double-crossed him. He sold the land that Librado wanted to another man.

They had to
walk about
a mile to
school, and
in the cold
weather
they did not
have clothes
that were
warm
enough.

Cesar E. Chavez

hall and service station that Librado had once owned. Richard and Cesar would go after school to pump gas and help out at the pool hall.

By 1937, the State of Arizona came to collect the taxes due on the Chavez farm. The state had granted them seven years to come up with the money. The taxes had accumulated to more than $4,000, and they were finally due. Librado had never been able to earn enough money to pay the taxes. Under the New Deal (a government program designed to help people who had lost money because of the Great Depression), Librado qualified for a loan. But the president of the bank, Archibald Griffin, was the wealthiest grower in the area. He wanted the Chavez farm for himself, so he blocked the loan. The state took legal possession of the ranch on August 29, 1937, but they did not evict the Chavez family right away. Librado continued to look for ways to pay the taxes he owed.

In August 1938 Librado left home with several relatives to look for work in California. They were told there was lots of work there, and he hoped to raise some money to save the farm. Thousands of people went to California looking for work during the Depression, but the rumors of opportunity were not true. There were more people looking for work than there were jobs. All Librado could find was a job in Oxnard, north of Los Angeles, thrashing beans. He found a little shack for the family in La Colonia, the poor part of town where the farm workers lived. He wrote to Juana telling her to come out with the children.

Juana packed up their five children. Two cousins drove the family to find Librado. When the family was reunited, they all sought work in the fields. Even the whole family working together could not make enough money to pay the rent where they lived. Librado decided to give up and return to Yuma and try once more to save the family farm.

In 1939 the State of Arizona finally held a public auction to sell the Chavez farm to pay the taxes. Only two people showed up at the auction: Librado and the wealthy banker-grower, Archibald Griffin. Librado had no money to bid for his land, but he bid anyway. His $2,300 bid was accepted by the state, and he was given thirty days to come up with the money. Of course, he still could not get a loan, so Mr. Griffin then won the rebid for $1,750. Under the Homestead Act, Librado could have gotten his land back by paying just the $1,750 that Griffin had paid for it, instead of the $4,000 he owed in taxes. But Librado still could not come up with that amount of money.

Rita and Cesar

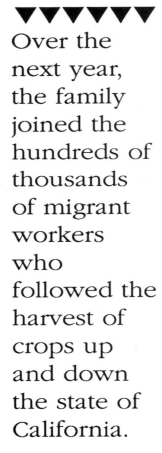

Over the next year, the family joined the hundreds of thousands of migrant workers who followed the harvest of crops up and down the state of California.

Cesar E. Chavez

Mr. Griffin sent someone with a big red tractor, who started to uproot trees. He bulldozed the land and the family was pushed off their farm. All the family could take with them was whatever they could fit into their car. Hungry and desperate, the Chavez family headed west in search of some way to make a living. Cesar was twelve at the time. His family arrived in San José, California, in late June to pick cherries. They had no place to stay.

Over the next year, the family joined the hundreds of thousands of migrant workers who followed the harvest of crops up and down the state of California. They lived in one-room tar-paper shacks, in tents, or in their car. In one year, Cesar estimated that he had been to more than thirty different schools. Cesar stopped going to school before he was able to finish eighth grade because his father needed him to work. He said it was much worse going to so many different schools in California than the stability he had when he was attending one school in Yuma. "I think the worst was not being noticed," Chavez said. "The schools treated you [as if] you didn't exist. Their indifference was incredible. When you went to school for the first time, the principal and the teacher would discuss where they should put you, right in front of you. It made you feel [as if] you weren't important."

CESAR E. CHAVEZ

The work of the migrant farm worker is very hard. Much of it is back-breaking stoop labor – they have to bend over all day in the fields to pick crops. At the time, wealthy growers would bring in workers from Mexico by the busload to pick the crops. These workers competed with American workers for the same jobs. The workers from Mexico found the pay to be much better than anything they could find in Mexico, and they were willing to work for very low wages. Because there were so many workers who wanted the same job, this drove the wages down even further.

Cesar's interest in labor unions began when his father and other relatives became members of many unions that were crushed by the growers. "About 1939, we were

This map of California shows some of the cities to which the Chavez family traveled.

living in San José," Cesar recalled in an interview for the *Farm Worker Press*. "One of the old CIO [Congress of Industrial Organizations] unions began organizing workers in the dried-fruit industry, so my father and uncle became members. Sometimes the men would meet at our house and I remember seeing their picket signs and hearing them talk. They had a strike and my father and uncle picketed at night. It made a deep impression on me. But of course they lost the strike, and that was the end of the union. [Wealthy growers would simply bring in more farm workers – strike-

Migrant workers bend over all day long to pick lettuce in the fields.

breakers – to pick the crops, and the strike would lose effect.] But from that time on, my father joined every new agricultural union that came along . . . and when I was nineteen I joined the National Agricultural Workers Union. But it didn't have any more success than any other of the farm workers' unions." Cesar recalled, however, that his family was always the first ones to leave the fields the minute anyone yelled *"Huelga!"* – which is Spanish for "Strike!"

Cesar E. Chavez

Librado Chavez was always looking for work for his family. He would drive around looking for people who could tell them what farm was hiring. The growers would hire recruiters or labor contractors, who would go out looking for migrant workers and tell them where the work was. They were paid a set amount of money for every family they sent to the farm. The workers were often told of work on a particular farm where they could earn a particular wage. The recruiters made it sound attractive. When the family arrived, they found the growers were paying only half of what was

Cesar's family was always among the first to leave the fields the minute anyone cried, *"Huelga!"*

promised. They would claim they had too many workers competing for the same jobs. If one family did not want the work, then another one would.

The first time the family picked peas, they learned a lot about the hopelessness of trying to earn a living as a migrant. All of the children in the Chavez family helped their parents pick the peas. They spent hours in the fields, bent over, filling their baskets. At the ends of the

At the end
of three
hours, the
entire
family had
earned only
twenty
cents
combined.

fields, the growers would weigh and sort the crop. They only paid for what they considered "good" peas. At the end of three hours, the entire family had earned only twenty cents combined.

When Cesar was fifteen, he met Helen Fabela. She had been born in Brawley, California. He met her when his family was looking for work near Delano. Cesar went into town one night and ended up in a snow-cone parlor called La Baratita. There were a lot of young people Cesar's age there, and Helen was among them. He learned that she worked in a nearby grocery store, and Cesar went there often to visit her. But this was in the middle of World War II, and in 1944, when he was seventeen, Cesar enlisted in the U.S. Navy. He served for two years, including time spent in the western Pacific at the end of the war.

When the war ended, Cesar rejoined his family and picked up his relationship with Helen. Helen and Cesar were married on October 22, 1948, in Reno, Nevada, and later had a church wedding in San José. Richard got married earlier that year, and Rita got married around the same time that Helen and Cesar did. Cesar then returned to Delano to pick grapes.

Helen and Cesar soon tired of living in a one-room shack in Delano. They had no electricity

or running water. They decided to move to San
José, where Richard was working on an apricot
farm. Cesar was able to get work there one or
two days a week. In 1949 Helen and Cesar had
their first son. They named him Fernando. Their
next child, Sylvia, was born in 1950. Eventually,
Helen and Cesar had eight children.

The whole Chavez clan moved to Greenfield
and rented a small farm together. They tried to
grow strawberries. After two years, they gave up.
Cesar and Richard eventually found work
in different lumber mills. Richard became
an apprentice carpenter and Cesar got a
job as a lumber handler. Cesar and his
family were living in a barrio called *Sal
Si Puedes.*

Cesar had been working in the apricot orchards near San José when he met
a white man named Fred Ross. Fred Ross
was a community organizer. He moved

Migrant workers often
lived in tents or tar-
paper shacks.

across California organizing in the barrios to set
up local chapters of the Community Service Organization (CSO), a social action, civil rights
group for Hispanics. He was looking for people
to help him when he heard about Cesar Chavez.
On June 9, 1952, Fred Ross went to visit Cesar.
When Cesar came home from work that evening,
Helen told him an Anglo had been by to see
him earlier that day. Cesar tried to avoid Fred

CESAR E. CHAVEZ

Ross. But Ross was persistent. He kept coming back. Finally, Cesar agreed to meet with him.

Fred Ross told Cesar he was an organizer for the Community Service Organization that was working with Mexican Americans in the cities. Fred did a good job of explaining how poor people could get together to change things. Cesar liked what he heard. He volunteered to help Ross get Mexican Americans registered to vote. Cesar understood very quickly that a whole group of people had much more power to change the course of events than individuals.

"I always have had, and I guess I always will have, a firm belief that if you muster enough power, you can move things, but it's all on the basis of power . . . it's unfortunate that power is needed to get justice. . . . We wanted to build power within a community in order to solve some of its problems. That meant building up political power by getting people registered to vote and organizing them. Unfortunately, many were not citizens. So Fred started a citizenship drive," Cesar recalled.

Soon Cesar lost his job. He went to work for the CSO full time. He learned how to organize people. He was only twenty-five years old at the time, but he was learning a lot that he would use later when he organized a union. He worked for the CSO from 1952 until 1962. Cesar found

Fred did a good job of explaining how poor people could get together to change things.

that he was good at organizing. He was named general director in 1958.

Many people in the CSO were farm workers, but the organization did not help them directly with their labor problems. If he had had the support of the CSO, Cesar said he would have started the union there. The CSO would not support Cesar's idea for a farm workers' union.

Finally, Cesar had to make a decision. He wanted to start a farm labor union with no strings attached. He knew there would be lots of frustrations, lots of difficulties, and tremendous challenges. He just had to try. He decided to resign from his decent-paying job as director with the CSO. With his own money, about $1,200 that Helen and he had managed to save over the past several years, Cesar Chavez founded the National Farm Workers Association. He convinced a woman named Dolores Huerta to give up her job with the CSO, too, and help him organize the NFWA. On September 30, 1962, Cesar called a union convention in an abandoned Fresno theater.

This photograph was taken in 1962 at the cofounding convention of the NFWA. Dolores Huerta is shown second from left. Cesar Chavez is on right.

The growers regularly called on the courts and the law enforcement agencies to protect their interests.

Cesar E. Chavez

Cesar had seen firsthand that the power of the growers was awesome. They could summon congressmen to pass laws favorable to them, and they blocked legislation that would have helped the farm workers. The growers regularly called on the courts and the law enforcement agencies to protect their interests. All of this led to exploitation of the farm worker. And the government allowed it to go on. The growers argued that in agriculture, they are defenseless during the harvest. If the workers were allowed to strike like other labor forces in the United States, they would effectively be holding a gun to the growers' heads. The workers would be in a position to threaten the entire crop. Therefore, agricultural labor had always been excluded from all labor laws protecting the rights of workers in all other industries to organize into unions that would improve their lives. So the endless exploitation of the workers continued, and they were powerless to do anything about it. Little by little, Cesar Chavez started organizing a union that would win rights for the farm workers.

Cesar's plan was to organize the union one member at a time, until they had enough members to have an effective voice. Then they would some day be strong enough to demand that the growers negotiate union contracts. If necessary, the union could go on strike. Cesar was up against insurmountable odds. For one hundred years, every farm labor union had been crushed by the growers.

While Cesar was organizing his union, Helen had to return to the fields to earn money to feed the family. She got up very early in the morning, made breakfast for all their children, made their lunches and left it for them, and then went to work. When she came home from work, she had to cook dinner and try to clean the house.

The children were very understanding and tried to help their parents. Some of the children would go with Helen to help in the fields. But, their youngest son, Anthony, always wanted to go with Cesar.

The Chavez family, from left to right: standing – Anna, Eloise, Sylvia, Helen, Cesar; sitting – Paul, Elizabeth, and Anthony. Missing from picture: Fernando and Linda.

Cesar worked eighteen or more hours every day. He would drive up and down the great central valley of California, often with Anthony, knocking on doors, stopping workers on the road or out in the fields. He distributed cards to farm workers, asking them how much money they thought they should be earning an hour. He was shocked to learn that many workers would be happy to make $1.10 to $1.25 an hour. (They were earning about $.90 an hour at the time.) Cesar thought they should be earning about $1.75 an hour.

Cesar refused all financial assistance for his union from the beginning. He wanted his members to fully support their own union, and he did not want to be indebted to anyone who might have other plans for his organization. He even turned down a private grant of $50,000. His brother Richard and cousin Manuel, who were working with him at the time, were not happy with Cesar about turning down this financial assistance. They even threatened to quit. But Cesar talked about forming an association of people who wanted a better life, and he did not want to be controlled by anyone.

By 1965, the National Farm Workers Association had about 1,700 families enrolled. Their union was growing. But he felt he needed about three more years to organize workers before he could take any real action for change in the fields. Unfortunately, the test of his union's strength came well before that.

In September 1965, the Agricultural Workers Organizing Committee, centered in Delano, went on strike for higher wages. Eight days later, the

▼▼▼▼▼▼

Cesar refused all financial assistance for his union from the beginning.

▲▲▲▲▲▲

Cesar E. Chavez

National Farm Workers Association voted to join the strike. The strike spread to include about two thousand workers in twenty farm labor camps. In some places, the growers locked the workers out of the camps, where the workers had been living for years. *La Huelga* – the Delano Grape Strike – had begun.

The growers were always angry whenever a strike was started. Sometimes they would send men with weapons to threaten or hurt the striking workers. Cesar Chavez was committed to fighting for his cause in a nonviolent manner. He did not like violence, and was taught as a young boy by his mother that violence was not the way to handle anything. He knew from reading about men like Mahatma Ghandi in India and the Reverend Martin Luther King, Jr., that with nonviolence comes strength and determination. Nonviolent movements for justice can win with time and patience. One of the nonviolent ways that Cesar chose to press for reform was the boycott. In a boycott, the workers ask the public not to buy or use a particular product. He started the first boycott against the products sold by a big wine grape grower, Schenley, in October 1965. If no one would buy the products, then the growers could not make any money. With the help of the public, Cesar believed the union

Cesar Chavez was committed to fighting for his cause in a nonviolent manner . . . One of the nonviolent ways Cesar chose to press for reform was the boycott.

could develop the economic power to counter that of the growers.

The strike went on and on with no resolution in sight. Cesar led a march from Delano to the steps of the state capitol in Sacramento in 1966. More than seventy people made the entire twenty-five-day march with Cesar, which on some days swelled to thousands of marchers. Governor Edmund G. (Pat) Brown was not there to meet them when they arrived to the applause of 10,000 union supporters. The march was successful, however. Along the way, they heard that Schenley was ready to negotiate. They signed a contract in June 1966, providing an hourly wage of $1.75, job protection for the workers, standby pay, and paid vacations. It was their first victory.

The NFWA marched from Delano to Sacramento, California, in March 1966.

Soon, the two striking unions merged into one led by Cesar Chavez. They voted to affiliate themselves with the AFL-CIO (American Federation of Labor – Congress of Industrial Organizations), becoming the United Farm Workers

Organizing Committee (UFWOC). The UFWOC soon won contracts with other major grape growers in the area. They were all wine-grape growers, however. The table-grape growers did not concede, and caused a much greater problem. Ninety percent of the table grapes consumed in the United States came from California. The wine-grape growers had been hurt by Cesar's boycott. But the struck table-grape growers began to market their produce under the labels of other growers. Cesar felt he had no choice but to take on the entire table-grape industry.

Cesar began a boycott of all California table or fresh grapes. He sent volunteer workers out to major cities throughout the United States and Canada to urge the people not to eat grapes. By the end of the year, they had managed to cut grape consumption by 20 percent.

As the strike dragged on, some of the workers became impatient. A few wanted to turn to more violent methods. But Cesar said no. He did

Senator Robert F. Kennedy is shown here on March 10, 1968, breaking the fast with Cesar Chavez. Also shown to left of Senator Kennedy is Helen Chavez and to right of Cesar is his mother, Juana Estrada Chavez.

not want one person to lose his life for *La Causa*. Instead, Cesar chose to go without any food to show the farm workers how important it was to win without violence. He would not eat for twenty-five days. He began his fast on February 14, 1968. Nearly ten thousand people were with Chavez when he ended the fast in Delano. They were from all religions, nationalities, and political backgrounds and included Senator Robert Kennedy. Senator Kennedy described Cesar as "one of the heroic figures of our time."

On July 29, 1970, Cesar Chavez and John Giumarra, Sr., signed a contract agreement that officially ended the five-year grape strike. Also shown in picture standing, from left to right: Manuel Uranday, Bishop Joseph Donnelley, Monsignor George Higgins, Jerry Sherry, editor of the *Catholic Monitor*, and John Giumarra, Jr.

But the strike went on. So did the frustration. Eventually, the boycott brought public support for the striking workers, and by July 1970 most of the table-grape growers had signed union contracts with the United Farm Workers Organizing Committee. Now 85 percent of all California grapes were being picked by union labor. The grape boycott was called off. The five-year strike and boycott had ended.

Within months, however, most lettuce and vegetable growers in California's Salinas Valley signed contracts with the Teamsters Union. It was a move designed to stop the workers from joining Cesar's UFW. About 10,000 vegetable workers in the Salinas Valley – most of the work force – walked out on strike under Cesar's leadership. Some growers signed UFW contracts after Cesar turned once more to the boycott. But the struggle went on with other growers for years.

By 1973, the gains Cesar had made in the grape vineyards were being eroded. Most of the grape producers would not renew their three-year contracts with United Farm Workers. The grape growers instead signed contracts with the Teamsters Union. The Teamsters signed "sweetheart" contracts. These contracts benefit employers more than workers. Most grape workers reacted by going on strike. More trouble followed. One of the farm workers, Juan de la Cruz, had been picketing at a vineyard south of Delano when he was shot down by rifle fire from a passing car. With the death of de la Cruz, violence flared up in the San Joaquin Valley. Another striker was killed. By 1973, the UFW had only twelve contracts left with growers; its membership shrank from 40,000 to 6,500.

Juan de la Cruz was shot to death on the picket line.

Cesar did not give up. He continued to do what was necessary. Now he not only had to fight the growers, but he also had to take on

CESAR E. CHAVEZ

the powerful Teamsters Union. He turned once more to the boycott and asked the consumers not to buy grapes, lettuce, and Gallo wine, which was being produced by a struck grape grower. A nationwide poll at the time showed seventeen million American adults supported the UFW by not buying grapes.

In 1975 Cesar enjoyed a major victory with the passage of the Agricultural Labor Relations Act, the nation's first law protecting and promoting the right of farm workers to organize. It was pushed through the California legislature by then Democratic Governor Edmund G. (Jerry) Brown, Jr. It provided for a five-member farm labor board to hear farm workers' grievances and to supervise elections. Growers could no longer get away with firing workers or refusing to negotiate union contracts in good faith.

Despite the setbacks and the slowness of the government to react, the UFW made progress. Tens of thousands of California farm workers voted for the union. Cesar negotiated many new contracts with the growers. Farm workers at unionized ranches enjoyed higher wages, complete family medical care, and many other benefits. Growers at nonunion farms were forced to treat their workers better out of fear that they too would join the UFW.

Deukmejian's political appointees refused to enforce the Agricultural Labor Relations Act.

CESAR E. CHAVEZ

When Republican Governor George Deukmejian was elected in 1982 with millions of dollars in campaign contributions from agricultural interests, Cesar saw most farm workers eventually lose the protection that the union contracts had brought. Deukmejian's political appointees refused to enforce the Agricultural Labor Relations Act. Many UFW contracts were lost. Trying to regain the momentum he once had, Chavez organized another grape boycott in 1984.

In 1988 Cesar embarked on one last fast, which lasted for thirty-six days, to call attention to the use of pesticides on the crops. But by now, Cesar was sixty-one years old and his doctor was concerned about his health. On the final day of the fast, Robert Kennedy's widow and some of her children came to Delano to celebrate mass and express their support for Cesar Chavez. Along with the Kennedys, the rest of the Chavez family and a group of celebrities, including actors Lou Diamond Phillips, Edward James Olmos, and Martin Sheen, stood by Cesar.

On August 21, 1988, Helen Chavez and Ethel Kennedy joined Cesar Chavez as he ended his fast. Cesar presented Jesse Jackson with a wooden cross. Fernando Chavez, Cesar's son, is shown to the right of Jesse Jackson.

The United Farm Workers of America has had many victories and setbacks over the years. It has won better wages and increased benefits, such as medical plans and retirement benefits. There are better working conditions today and grievance procedures are set up to protect farm workers who labor under union contracts. Until he died in 1993, Cesar Chavez continued with the overall planning and strategy of the United Farm Workers. He spoke to many groups and walked picket lines all across the country.

Cesar worked to get justice for farm workers right up until the day he died. He traveled across the country and to other countries to talk about *La Causa* and to help people understand the tactics of organizing nonviolently to create change for the better.

Since 1972 Cesar had lived with his family at La Paz in Keene, California, the union's headquarters in Kern County's Tehachapi Mountains. Like other UFW officers and staff, he was a volunteer and received subsistence pay that never amounted to more than $5,000 per year. "How can you help poor people if you don't know what it is to be poor?" he would say.

Cesar E. Chavez passed away in his sleep on April 23, 1993, at the age of sixty-six. More than fifty thousand people attended Cesar's funeral at Delano. He was laid to rest at La Paz in

Arturo Rodriguez took over the leadership of the UFW after Cesar's death.

CESAR E. CHAVEZ

his rose garden at the foot of the hill he would often climb to watch the sunrise.

Many skeptics declared that the union was dead after Cesar passed away. This could not be further from the truth. On Cesar's birthday, March 31, 1994, under the leadership of Cesar's son-in-law and successor as union president,

Arturo S. Rodriguez, the UFW marched three-hundred forty-three miles from Delano to Sacramento, echoing Cesar's historic 1966 pilgrimage. The marchers demonstrated the strength of the UFW and the fact that Cesar's dream of a national union for farm workers remains a possibility. There were more than fifteen thousand people waiting at the end of the march to Sacramento. The UFW continues to win elections and negotiate contracts for farm workers.

Cesar left a legacy that was much more than a union. The National Farm Worker Service Center, run by Cesar's son Paul, builds high-quality houses that farm workers and other poor people

In 1994 Pres. Bill Clinton presented Cesar Chavez with the Presidential Medal of Freedom. From left to right, front row: Sylvia Chavez Delgado, Barbara Ybarra (granddaughter), Linda Chavez Rodriguez and husband, Arturo, Helen, Pres. Clinton and wife Hillary, Dolores Huerta, Olivia Rodriguez (granddaughter), and Magdaleno M. Rose-Avila, the executive director of the Chavez Foundation.

Cesar E. Chavez

can afford to buy. Anthony Chavez runs a growing network of radio stations called *Radio Campesina* (farm worker radio). Cesar's daughters Liz and Linda operate Farm Worker Corporation, which manages money for the entire movement. There is a pension fund to provide money for union members when they retire, and a medical insurance program for farm workers working under UFW contracts. There is also a credit union (bank), a kitchen and dining hall, an auto shop, and a print shop at La Paz. More than seventy people live there all year, and during the summer, many college students come to La Paz to volunteer and learn about Cesar's work.

In 1991 Cesar received the Aguila Azteca (Aztec Eagle), Mexico's highest award given to people of Mexican heritage who have made major contributions outside of Mexico. On August 8, 1994, Cesar became the first Mexican American to receive the Presidential Medal of Freedom, the highest civilian honor in the United States. When he presented the award posthumously to Helen Chavez, President Bill Clinton said, "He was for his own people a Moses figure. The farm workers who labored in the field and yearned for respect and self-sufficiency pined their hopes on this remarkable man who, with faith and discipline, with soft-spoken humility and amazing inner strength, led a very courageous life." Helen

Cesar left a legacy that was much more than a union.

CESAR E. CHAVEZ

Chavez and six of their eight children traveled to the White House to receive the honor.

In 1994 Cesar's family and the officers of the UFW created the Cesar E. Chavez Foundation to inspire current and future generations by promoting the ideals of Cesar's life, work, and vision. The Foundation's headquarters is at La Paz, the future location of the Cesar E. Chavez Library and the Cesar E. Chavez Training and Education Center. People come to visit Cesar's grave and to learn about his legacy.

Even though Cesar never finished the eighth grade, he never stopped learning. In a 1984 address to the Commonwealth Club of San Francisco, Cesar said, "You cannot uneducate the person who has learned to read. You cannot humiliate the person who feels pride. You cannot oppress people who are not afraid of anyone."

Cesar Chavez taken in 1988 with Gina Ortiz, daughter of Frank Ortiz, the former executive board member of the UFW and Anthony Chavez, Paul's first-born son

This story has been reviewed for historical accuracy by the Cesar E. Chavez Foundation; it contains information and photographs supplied to the author, courtesy of the Foundation. For additional information about Cesar E. Chavez, contact:
The Cesar E. Chavez Foundation
P.O. Box 62, Keene, CA 93531
805-822-5571
chavezfdtn@igc.apc.org

ANTONIA NOVELLO

Doctor, Former Surgeon General

1944-

> **"I** have very little tolerance [for] people who complain of being sick and truly are not, or who use sickness as their piggyback for not doing what they are supposed to do. **"**

"Antonia Novello: A Dream Come True," *Saturday Evening Post*, May/June 1991.

BIO HIGHLIGHTS

- Born Antonia Coello on August 23, 1944, in Fajardo, Puerto Rico; mother: Ana Delia Coello; father: Antonio Coello
- Born with defective large intestine; spent many years as a sick child, in and out of hospitals
- At eighteen, finally had surgery to correct the painful defect
- Graduated from University of Puerto Rico in Rio Piedras in 1965 with B.S. degree
- Received M.D. degree from University of Puerto Rico, San Juan in 1970
- Married Joseph Novello, 1970
- Intern and residency at University of Michigan
- 1976, starts private practice
- 1978, closes private practice and enters public health
- Staff physician at National Institutes of Health, 1979-1980
- Executive secretary in Division of Research Grants, 1981-1986
- 1982, earned master's degree in public health from Johns Hopkins University in Baltimore, Maryland
- Nominated by President George Bush on October 17, 1989, to be surgeon general
- March 9, 1990, sworn in as fourteenth U.S. Surgeon General. Became first female, first Puerto Rican, and first Latina U.S. Surgeon General
- Currently: special representative for Health and Nutrition at UNICEF; resides with her husband in Washington, D.C.

When
Antonia
Novello was
a little girl,
she
dreamed of
being a
pediatrician.

ANTONIA NOVELLO

When Antonia Novello was a little girl, she dreamed of being a pediatrician. She liked to imagine herself as a doctor for the little kids in her hometown. But she never told anyone she wanted to be a doctor. "It seemed too grand a notion," Dr. Novello said. Like many other girls growing up, she was afraid of failing. What if she told everyone that she wanted to be a doctor but then never became one? Better to keep her secret to herself.

Antonia Coello was born on August 23, 1944, in the small town of Fajardo, Puerto Rico. She was the oldest of three children born to Antonio and Ana Delia Coello. Her father was a schoolteacher; he died when Antonia was eight years old. Her mother, who later remarried, was a principal of a junior high school in Fajardo for thirty years. Antonia grew up with her mother and stepfather, Ramon Flores, who was an electrician.

Antonia was born with a congenital defect of the large intestine. Her colon was abnormally large and it did not work very well. It caused "Tonita," as she was called as a child, a lot of pain. Every summer, she was hospitalized for at least two weeks. She was promised that she could have surgery to correct the defect, but no one ever got around to it. "Somebody forgot," Antonia said. "The university hospital was in the north, I was thirty-two miles away, my mother could only take me on Saturdays, so the surgery was never done." Year after year she suffered. "I was a sick kid," Antonia remembered, "although my mother never made me feel sick." Because her mother never pitied her, Antonia never really felt sorry for herself. Her doctors became her friends.

"My pediatrician and my gastroenterologist were so nurturing and good to me that doctors became my buddies," Antonia recalled. "My pediatrician was kind. I wanted to be a doctor like him. My gastroenterologist was the dean of the medical school, and all my life his was the hand I saw – soothing and caring. And my favorite aunt was my nurse; she always said, 'You have to be a doctor.'" So, Antonia vowed she would become a doctor when she grew up so that other children would not have to suffer like she did. "I do believe that some people fall through the cracks. I was one of those," she said.

When Antonia was eighteen, she convinced her mother that she needed to have the surgery to correct the painful defect. It was difficult to find a doctor willing to perform the operation. The only doctor they found was a cardiovascular surgeon, who normally performed surgery on the heart and blood vessels. He was willing to give it a try. There were complications after the

▼▼▼▼▼

"I do believe that some people fall through the cracks. I was one of those."

▲▲▲▲▲

Her constant illness made her aware of how others might suffer when they are sick.

ANTONIA NOVELLO

surgery. Antonia had to leave Puerto Rico for the United States. She checked into the Mayo Clinic in Minnesota for two months. The doctors at the Mayo Clinic were able to correct the problem. Finally, Antonia was free from pain. She wanted to make sure that others would not have to wait eighteen years for a necessary operation. Her constant illness made her aware of how others might suffer when they are sick.

Ana Coello Flores encouraged her daughter to continue with her education as far as she could. She would not let Antonia work while she was in school because she was afraid that Antonia would be sidetracked by material rewards before she got to her "real job." After graduating from high school, Antonia enrolled at the University of Puerto Rico in Rio Piedras, as a pre-medical student. She earned her Bachelor of Science degree in 1965. Because there were only sixty-five people per class at the University of Puerto Rico Medical School, Antonia did not tell her mother she had applied until after she was accepted. She was afraid she would not get in. She was also worried about where the money would come from. Her mother and stepfather were not wealthy, but they did support her career choice. "When I told her I was accepted to medical school," Antonia recalls, "she said, 'As long as there is a bank out there, we will find your tuition.'"

Antonia earned her Medical Doctor degree from the University of Puerto Rico, San Juan in 1970. In that same year, she married another doctor, Joseph Novello, who was then a Navy flight surgeon stationed in Fajardo. Together they moved to Michigan, where they both continued their medical studies. She did her intern and residency in pediatrics at the University of Michigan in Ann Arbor, and Joe continued his studies in psychiatry. In 1971 she was chosen Intern of the Year. A classmate of Antonia, Dr. Samuel Sefton, who later became a neonatologist in Kalamazoo, Michigan, said, "[Antonia] was a resident when female physicians weren't as readily accepted as they are today. . . . She was a wonderful physician, and she was warm, friendly, and well-respected."

During her two-year residency, Antonia's favorite aunt died of kidney failure; Antonia was also hospitalized with a severe kidney ailment. As a result of these events, Antonia decided to study pediatric nephrology (concerning the kidneys), first at the University of Michigan until 1974, and then at Georgetown University Hospital in Washington, D.C. from 1974 to 1975.

In 1976 Antonia was ready to start on her own. She opened her own private practice in

During her two-year residency, Antonia's favorite aunt died of kidney failure.

ANTONIA NOVELLO

Springfield, Virginia, where she specialized in pediatrics and nephrology. After two short years, however, she decided to close her practice. "When the pediatrician cries as much as the parents [of patients] do, it is time to get out," she said.

In 1978 Antonia entered public health, where she has since made her lifelong career. She was hired as a project officer in the artificial kidney and chronic uremia program at the National Institutes of Health. She was a staff physician at the National Institutes of Health from 1979 through 1980 and the executive secretary in the Division of Research Grants from 1981 through 1986. In 1982 and 1983, Antonia was a Congressional fellow on the staff of the Labor and Human Resources Committee, which was chaired by Senator Orrin Hatch from Utah. In 1982 she earned a master's degree in public health from Johns Hopkins University in Baltimore, Maryland. From 1986 until 1989, she was deputy director of the National Institute of Child Health and Human Development.

Dr. Novello was very happy with her progression through the U.S. Public Health Service. She thought that when she became deputy director, she would be at the peak of her career. She did not know what to expect next. But there were greater things ahead. On October 17, 1989, Presi-

In 1978, Antonia entered public health, where she has since made her lifelong career.

dent George Bush nominated Antonia Novello to be the next surgeon general, the nation's chief adviser on matters of public health.

In 1990 Antonia Novello made history when she was sworn in as the fourteenth surgeon general of the United States. Antonia became the first female, the first Puerto Rican, and the first Latina U.S. Surgeon General. She had become a doctor of all the people. At her swearing-in ceremony, held on March 9, 1990, in the Roosevelt Room of the White House, Dr.

Antonia Novello is sworn in as the new surgeon general by President George Bush.

Novello confirmed what many of us wanted to hear when she said, "The American dream is alive and well today."

Being the surgeon general was a big responsibility. The overall mission of the surgeon general is the protection, improvement, and advancement of the health of all American people. The surgeon general is also a spokesperson for the President on health issues. The surgeon general commissions research focusing on major health problems and gives warnings to the public about dangers to health. Dr. Novello was also charged with overseeing the 6,400-member active-duty commissioned corps of the United States Public Health Service. Members of the corps staff health centers around the country, on Native American reservations, and in other places in the United States where there are medical personnel shortages.

Shortly after Dr. Novello became the U.S. Surgeon General, she traveled back to Puerto Rico. "When I got off the plane, kids from my mother's school lined both sides of the road handing me flowers. . . . I went to the VA hospital to speak. When the veterans saw my gold braid [she is a Vice Admiral in the Public Health Service] they all stood and saluted. . . . I realized that for these people, for women, I have to be good as a doctor, I have to be good as a surgeon general, I have to be everything."

Antonia returned to the United States and spent the first year as surgeon general listening and studying. In her second year, she launched several major campaigns that dealt with problems of children and young adults. She was particularly disturbed by the statistics surrounding smoking in the United States. The surgeon general had been warning the public about the dangers of smoking for nearly thirty years. That warning continues today. Yet millions of young people still smoke. Thousands start the habit every day. Studies have shown that 90 percent of adult smokers began smoking when they were children or young adults. "If the current rate of smoking among adults were to continue . . . ," Dr. Novello said in 1991, "then at least five million children now living in the United States will [eventually] die of smoking-related diseases." Dr. Novello felt that the tobacco industry should not be allowed to target children in their cigarette advertising. In 1992, Dr. Novello made headlines when she and James S. Todd, the executive vice president of the American Medical Association, held a news conference to urge R.J. Reynolds Tobacco Company to get rid of its ads that used a cartoon character, Joe Camel, to sell its cigarette products. It was also particularly disturbing to Dr. Novello that lung cancer had recently surpassed breast cancer as the number-one cause of cancer deaths in women. It didn't seem that the American public was paying attention to the health warnings issued by the surgeon general.

During a press conference in Washington, Antonia called for the removal of all advertising featuring the "Old Joe Camel" cartoon character.

She was concerned that most young drinkers do not understand that beer and wine coolers are potent alcoholic beverages. Antonia said when she spoke on college campuses and told

When she spoke on college campuses and told the students that beer was alcoholic, they thought she was just being funny!

the students that beer was alcoholic, they thought she was just being funny!

Dr. Novello was also dismayed at how many children were not being immunized against common childhood diseases. "Children ages two to four have the greatest number of cases of measles," she said, "and it is not because of a lack of vaccine."

Dr. Novello also brought to light the special health concerns of Hispanic Americans. She noted that they lacked health care coverage in large numbers and a disproportionate number fall victim to AIDS, high blood pressure, diabetes, kidney disease, and various cancers.

When Dr. Novello was surgeon general, she made it well known that she had a special affection for children. She visited many young patients in hospitals and tried to take some time to cheer them up. Her office was decorated with Cabbage Patch dolls, children's artwork, photos of youngsters, and a collage of messages from Puerto Rican schoolchildren. Some commented that it looked more like a pediatrician's waiting room than a bureaucrat's office!

When President Bill Clinton was elected, Dr. Novello was appointed as the United Nations International Children's Fund (UNICEF) Special Representative for Health and Nutrition for Women, Children, and Youth. In this job, she works toward the immunization of all children worldwide and for the prevention of alcohol, tobacco, and other drug abuse. She spends two days a week in the New York UNICEF office, and the rest of the week in her Washington, D.C., office.

Dr. Novello and her husband, Joe, live in the Washington, D.C., area with their cat, Nicolosa. Dr. Novello often takes time out to look at the humorous side of things. "I survived many times in my life by learning to laugh at myself – that's the best medicine," she said. And her humorous side gets even funnier when she is in the presence of her brother-in-law, Don Novello, a comedian who has played Father Guido Sarducci on *Saturday Night Live*. "For the longest time, we didn't want Donnie to admit he was related to us," jokes Antonia.

Back to the serious side, Dr. Novello feels she has learned a lot about being a good doctor from spending the first twenty years of her life as a sick person and the latter part in public health: "I have very little tolerance [for] people who complain of being sick and truly are not, or who use sickness as their piggyback for not doing what they are supposed to do. And I have very little tolerance for people who say they can't do something or they can't get to the top, because believe me, if I did it . . . it can be done."

"I have survived many times in my life by learning to laugh at myself . . ."

Index